Naughty Narratives

Karmel Poet

Naughty Narratives
Copyright © 2017 by Karmel Poet

Cover Art provided by: Maduranga

Table of Contents

My Disclaimer

I am like the energizer bunny
I go hard in the paint
I am the bedroom bully
And I
Will make you faint
If you can't handle my body and give me all that I
need
I will drain you of your DNA
Take all of your seed
I'm not responsible if my sex makes you lose your
mind
That's my disclaimer
Here
Sign on the dotted line
You want to step up and say you want a taste
Saying you can put this poetic pussy in its place
Its place is on your tongue
Or your dick once it's nice and hard
I promise to be gentle
You can let down your guard
I won't hurt you
At least not much
And even if I do
You'll still be craving my touch
The touch of my hands
My mouth
My cat

Soon as I leave
You'll be calling me to come back
Wanting some more of this cowgirl action
Saying you've never had this kind of satisfaction
The way my hands moved while I was gripping you
Or the sounds of my moans while you did what you
do
You weren't ready for me to jump on take charge
You said other chicks got scared because you were
so large
Well
I aint never scared
And I won't run
Although you might want to before I'm done
Don't worry
When your dick is tired
I won't complain
Just replace it with your tongue and do more of the
same
I can ride your face until I get mine
Or we can switch it up
And do sixty-nine
Although once my mouth gets to working down
south
You might not be able to do much with your mouth
Except moan
And tell me how good I am
Lay back with your eyes closed and try to plan
A way

To keep this good stuff all to yourself
Wanting to keep my mouth and cat up on a shelf
But you can't handle it
Not on your own
While you're sleeping it off
I'm on my way home
Because this poetic pussy is too much for you to
tame
I proved that when I made you scream my name
You are more than welcome to try again
When it's over
You can bow down to the queen of pussy and pen
I won't tell anybody that I made you tap out
Although
I think your neighbors did hear you shout
Maybe next time I won't use my tongue
Because my head game will definitely have you
sprung
I'll just lie on the bed or maybe stand in the shower
You want me to tap out
You better have some power
Better be able to pick me up and give it to me up
against the wall
You want to satisfy me
Then you better give your all
See
I'll take what I want if it's worth the sweat
And I haven't met a man that can make me tap
out yet

So if you think you can do it
Step into the ring
Because if you knock me out
You are definitely a Clit King

Frustrated

Baby don't you know that I'm frustrated too
And I can't even get the release that you do
It's just not the same
Touching myself
I need you here to give me some help
But circumstances won't allow that right now
So I have to suffer through it
Somehow
My problem is that I have a very vivid imagination
Which makes this an even more difficult situation
I can imagine you saying things meant to tease
And me pushing you up against the wall
Then dropping to my knees
Setting you free and starting to lick
Until the head is nice and slick
Then standing up and turning around
Bending over so that you can get down
Or maybe having you drive to a deserted rest stop
Telling you to stay in your seat while I climb on top
Putting my breasts in your mouth as I ride
You making me so wet that you start to slide
In and out as the car starts to rock
And as I get close to the edge
There comes a knock
On my bedroom door and the vision is gone
I realize that I'm lying in my bed all alone

I can't wait for the day that we make our dreams
come true
Believe me when I say that I
Am just as frustrated as you

More

The storm brought you to me and that was just fine
We would only have one night because you were
not mine
You tried to play the role
Like sex wasn't why you came
But we both knew that our desires were the same
I had wanted you for so long I was not going to say
no
And you were so horny that you couldn't take it slow
You let me play with it first and make it hard as a
brick
Then I got on and showed you that I knew how to
drive a stick
You sucked and kissed on my nipples
You did it just right
I would've had no problem with you doing that all
night
You had other plans
So of course you switched it up
But that was after you had me wet enough to fill a
cup
Multiple orgasms from your dick tongue and hands
This is why I wanted you to be my man
I knew you'd be good
That you weren't all talk
That once you were done with me
I wouldn't be able to walk

You flipped me off of you
My time on top was done
My legs went on your shoulders
I definitely couldn't run
I was biting and scratching and rubbing on your head
While you were letting me know that you were the king in that bed
You caused my juices to run out of me and on to the sheet
My pussy must've been bad the way it was gettin' beat
I enjoyed every minute of it
You were comin' on strong
I just wish I would've known it wasn't going to last long
When you said you were done I wanted to scream
See
We had went multiple rounds in every one of my dreams
When we were done
I never told you what I was so mad at you for
It's because one round wasn't enough
I really wanted more

Teacher's Pet

I sit here
Squirming in my seat
But nothing can stop
That moist heat
Cumming from between my thighs
Every time I look into his eyes
And his voice is causing small earthquakes
I don't know how much more I can take
I just want to run my fingers through his hair
While straddling him in his chair
I can't seem to take my eyes off his lips
And I keep wanting to reach out and grab his hips
Every step he takes is pure poetry
He has no idea exactly HOW he inspires me
If he could read my mind
He'd probably blush
Maybe even end the class in a rush
He has no idea that he's caused this fire
I've become a pro at hiding my desire
He doesn't know that I pay such close attention
Because I'm having thoughts that I can't mention
Thoughts that cause me such distress
Like how I'd like him to bend me over his desk
So that I can take his DICtation
While earning an A in participation
Or maybe me being his lunchtime snack
While I'm on his desk on my back

You know
Karmel is a special treat
And I've been told I taste exceptionally sweet
Maybe he'd like it if we played a little game
And I was Lewinsky without the dress stain
I spend most of class with these visions in my head
Wondering if he's this passionate in bed
Plotting ways to get his head in my hands
While at full attention he happily stands
Unfortunately
He's my professor not even a friend
I really hate that this semester has to end
But then again
Maybe that's a good thing
Maybe he's been thinking about ways to make my
body sing
And just waiting for us both to be free
From the rules separating him
And me
Those rules that keep him just out of my reach
That keep him from learning the things I'd like to
teach
Like
How to make me cum
Or say his name
Or how to shake the screws out of his bed frame
While learning all of my various sex faces
He'll be very happy that student and teacher have
switched places

Because the things I'll demonstrate
Will be for his pleasure
And help him release all of that pent up pressure
That he's held onto the whole semester through
He'll finally learn
That I
Am a very passionate teacher too

One Helluva Ride

I closed the windows and locked the doors
Got in the middle of the bed
Down on all fours
I looked back and purred
Giving him a sexy smile
And said
Cum get this loving
Doggy style
He stood watching me before he came near
Then got on the bed and whispered in my ear
You know I like to get it from the back
I get so hard seeing you like that
I didn't answer
Just reached out my hand
And started to stroke and caress my man
He climbed on the bed and began to kiss that spot
The one on the back of my neck that gets me
instantly hot
He played with my nipples while I played with him
Once I was wet enough
He slid right in
This wasn't about lovemaking
It was time to fuck
He rode me like a bronco and I continued to buck
He was slapping my ass and pulling my hair
It was getting kinda rough but I didn't care
My legs started shaking

But I wasn't gonna fall
To hurry him along
I started clenching my walls
I kept throwing it back like I was trying to throw him
off
Then I felt him explode and he slowly went soft
I eased onto my stomach as he collapsed by my
side
And said between breaths
That was one helluva ride

Rainfall

The steady rhythm from the rain
Caused a desire she just
Couldn't contain
The moisture falling from the skies
Increased the wetness between her thighs
The storm put her mind in a zone
To want to make
And be made
To moan
The problem was
She didn't have a man
Just her imagination
And her hands
She tried to ignore the urges
But the rain kept falling
And there was no one there to hear her body
calling
So she did something she had never done before
She closed her eyes and let her hands explore
Her explorations started off a little slow
Because this was her first time
And she
Really didn't know
The steps to take to ensure she'd be pleased
She'd always had a man to tend to her needs
But
She was alone

And the rain made her hot

So

She worked until she found the right spot

She realized she was making sounds normally accompanied by squeaky springs

Yet she was at a point where she didn't mind not having those things

She had finally learned how to answer her body's call

And create floods from her own personal rainfall

The Kiss

He touched me
Held me
Lips caressed mine
Arms
Enveloped me from behind
So I turned
To give him full access
Craving so much more than just a simple caress
He kissed me
It started as a flutter across my lips
His tongue darting out
Taking little licks
Obviously he liked the taste
Because his tongue became a key
That easily unlocked me
I lost all thought of time
Forgot where I was and why
Nothing existed except he and I
His lips never left me but my clothes did
No part of me from him was hid
From my lips he slowly made his way south
Generous and attentive
He lingered over every part
I swear he was trying to taste my heart
The way he kissed my breasts
He could've stopped there and I would've been
satisfied

He was the moon controlling my tide
My waters rose and fell to the rhythm of his lips
He moved lower at a leisurely pace
Ignoring my pleas to please
He mumbled this isn't a race
Taking slow laps around my navel
He saturated my sheets
Had me panting from the heat
He created
Because his lips had still not left my body
This
Was the same kiss
From lips
To neck
To navel
Not one spot had he missed
He finally reached my lower lips
I wanted to run
But he gripped my hips
And drank like a man dying of thirst
I thought about tapping out
But
 This was only the first
Kiss
There would be plenty more
He drowned my kitten and made my body soar
On currents of unexplainable bliss
I still get weak every time I think of that kiss

Show and Prove

For you to be called King
It takes more than just a crown
You have to show and prove that you can put it
down
Poetic Pussy is not just for any man
We'll have you crawling away
Unable to stand
See
They call me Karmel because my pussy's so sweet
You'll be begging for more once you taste this treat
And you can have it
If you've got good tongue action
Because I don't play when it comes to my sexual
satisfaction
The good girl in me sleeps when Karmel comes out
to play
I hope you can handle me
If not
Be on your way
This isn't for rookies or the faint of heart
Be sure that you can finish before you even start
I like getting head
And I can give in return
I'm damned good at it too
As you will soon learn
I start off slow
Just licking the tip

Tasting and teasing
Making you want to flip
Then I take it further
And put the head in my mouth
Sucking with gentle pressure making
You want to shout
While playing with your pipe
And rubbing on your balls
My mouth makes you anxious to feel my inner walls
But not yet
I want to taste that first explosion
Then I'll ride your face while your dick is reloading
I hope you're ready for more because I am not
through
It's time for you to show me that your title
Clit King
Is true
Your face is a little sticky but you don't have to
move
I'll slide back and jump on that dick
You'll enjoy my groove
You won't be able to catch my rhythm but you
won't mind
Whenever you think you've got it
I'll switch it up every time
Don't worry
I'll let you take control in a minute
You just better be sure you can handle this while
you're up in it

I need you to do things to me to make my body sing
Or else you can no longer be called a Clit King

Storm Racers

The storm was the music used for their dance
The shaking from the thunder only served to
enhance
The vibrations
They were causing
As they moved together
This was the reason that they loved this type of
weather
No need for candles as the lighting flashed all
around
No need to be quiet
The thunder masked the sounds
While the storm intimidated some and had others
afraid
They were like two kids who freely played
They played in the bed
They played on the floor
The strength of the storm made them want to play
more
He was hungry for a meal that only she could
provide
He was the only horse around for her to ride
As long as the rain continued falling
He made sure that his name she was calling
And she returned the favor as they tossed and
turned
Using every single thing that she had ever learned

About how to please him

While trying new things

Loving the freedom that the storms always bring

Moans and screams

Scratches and sweat

This would be a storm they wouldn't soon forget

As the wind quieted and the drops began to slow

They moved back to the bed for their final crescendo

As the storm was ending

So were they

Covered in salty rain

Together they lay

Satisfied for the moment

Shaking yet warm

Already thinking of the next time they could race a storm

Good girl

i wear his collar with pride
Stand silently by His side
Eyes downcast
The way Daddy likes
When He speaks
i leak
With anticipation
Of His commands
But i must continue to stand
Testing my patience is part of His plan
And i understand
my role
But it's hard to control
my desire
His scent sparks a fire
That His voice stirs
i purr
Shit
Wasn't supposed to make a sound
He slowly turns around
Taps His wrist
Now i must wait
While He masturbates
Can't taste
That sweet cum
He knows i want sum
But while we're here

i
Must adhere
To the rules
Play it cool
See
This
Is business
And i must remain
His submissive misses

Another

Who are you
What did you do
Why can't I stop thinking about you
Why can't I forget how you made me feel
This must be a dream
It can't be real
Your touch on my skin
Smoother than silk
The taste of your skin
Sweeter than mother's milk
And nourishes my body just the same
Thinking of you makes me forget my name
Then I hear you say it in my mind
And it takes me back to the last time
We were together
It felt like a dream
The feeling couldn't have been as exquisite as it
seemed
The ecstasy you caused
The absolute bliss
No one has ever made me feel like this
The way your hands moved
Gentle and slow
Causing dams to break
And rivers to flow
And the things that you did with your tongue
Touching secret places rarely seen by anyone

You loved me so thoroughly in that situation
That I was already well satisfied by the time of
penetration
Just thinking about it brings a sexy smile to my face
But that's a story for another time
Another place

Travellers

You please me
Easily
The way you
Do
The things
You do
I can't help but moan
When you get on
Or should I say
In
Every match you win
The prize
Waves crashing between my thighs
Curses and sighs
That causes your nature to once again
Rise
The way you work your tongue
Makes me want to run
But loving your taste
Keeps me in place
The sounds that you make
Turn my tremors to full blown quakes
No way to explain
Impossible to contain
Feeling you throb
Always does its job
Causing vibrations

Immense saturation
Satiation
With no hesitation
Together
We arrive at our destination

Punishment

Come here baby
you've been a bad boy
So for your punishment
you get to be my toy
First order of business
Down on your knees
you will do as you're told until I am well pleased
But before you kneel
Get undressed
If you keep your clothes on
There'll be a mess
Now it's time for you to bow before your queen
Go treasure hunting and make me scream
Tease the pearl
Create tidal waves
Give me all the pleasure that I crave
You can't stop until I say so
So keep on making my juices flow
Let my wetness run down your chin
As you create explosions
Again and again
This is your punishment
Remember
It's all about me
I want to be blinded by the sensations
I don't need to see
I don't need my eyes to give commands

And my body will tell me if you understand
I know you're getting tired and you need to catch
your breath
But I'm not tired
So you can't rest
Why don't you stand up
Be careful
Don't fall
Now pick me up and give it to me up against the
wall
Not too hard
I want those strokes slow and strong
If you do it right
We won't be here for long
Mmmmmmmm
That's it baby
I like it like that
See
I knew you knew how to act
But you're still in trouble
So don't put me down
I want to hear you make some ooh ahh sounds
Now
Show me just how strong you are
Walk us to the bed
It's not far
It's time for me to take my toy for a ride
While your mouth to my mounds are applied
That's it baby

Don't they taste good
Keep following instructions like a good boy should
Your punishment's almost over
I'm almost done
As I increase my pace
I'm ready for you to cum
Look at me
I want to watch while you explode
I promise you are the best toy I've ever rode
This was definitely time well spent
And I thoroughly enjoyed
your punishment

Body Shots

The only licker I need
Is you
Make me feel drunk from the things you do
With your tongue
Have me sprung
From its
Flicker
But first
Let me satisfy my thirst
Or should I say taste
For you
Let me show you
What my tongue can do
Let me see
If I can taste your pulse
At the base of your neck
Don't try to keep it in check
There's that increase
But it's gonna get faster
See
I know you like it when I tease your nipples
Don't fight it
Go ahead and moan
I won't move
Until you do
I love the salty sweetness of you
And I could linger here

All day
This isn't just foreplay
This is me memorizing your skin with my tongue
While leaving my mark
Every time I lick my lips
In your presence
You'll remember
Out of your presence
I'll still taste your essence
And it'll spark a memory
Of me
Getting drunk
Off you
But I'm not through
I love the way your abs shake
As I make
My way
Lower
Going slower
So as to savor
Your flavor
I feel you
Pulsing beneath me
Wanting to greet me
But I'm not there yet
There are parts of you
I still haven't wet
But you can bet
That when I get

To where you want me
I am going to drive you crazy
See
Alcohol doesn't faze me
But you
Get me more than tipsy
When you allow me
To lick thee
Here
There
Everywhere
Patron can't get me gone
Like letting my tongue roam
Gin don't make my head swim
Like the taste of your skin
Wine won't make lose time
Like making you tongue-tied
Everybody's got their habits and addictions
Mine just happens to be the friction
Caused between tongue and skin
Damn
Those body shots always do me in

Intoxication
Collaboration with Nathan P.

KP:
Cooler than the other side of the pillow...
He approached me...
Inspiring thoughts of
I want to be drafted...
So he can coach me...
On how to create such heat...
While remaining so cool...
He...
And Billy Dee...
Must've went to the same school
Of style...
Then he smiled...
And I knew my clothes would only be on for a little
while...
Longer...
When he spoke
The desire just got stronger...
His baritone...
Became a metronome...
Ticking off the beats...
As I imagined us
Between the sheets...
My very vivid imagination...
Made it hard to focus on the conversation...
My school girl giggles...

And flirtatious wiggles...
Relayed my message just fine...
He extended his hand, the perfect gentleman...
Then invited me to his place for dinner and wine...

NP:
Billy Dee comparisons pinstripe suit me fine...
But I draw the line at Colt45...
Instead offering her a fine glass of wine...
Which I'm smoother than...
And when she took my hand..
She could tell I was a gentleman...
With hidden desires.....
Fueled by the heat of the infamous Aries fire....
I wanted her....
And wanted her to want me....
Hoping that we could partake of intimacies between the sheets...
The way she batted her almond shaped eyes...
Leaned in close to talk with her hand resting on my thighs...
Or at the sound of my voice she'd exhale a soft sigh....
Seemed like tell-tale signs....
But alas I didn't rush in....
Because while I desire her...
My desire is not to offend...

KP:

His debonair ways...

Had me in a daze...

Mind clouded in a haze...

He was what I craved...

And I was tired of playing coy...

Had to employ...

New strategies...

Fed him from my plate...

And didn't hesitate...

To swirl the wine with my tongue

While making eye contact...

Complimented him on the taste...

Intentionally bumping his waist...

With mine...

Hope he gets the message this time...

NP:

Never been good at making the first move...

But expertly skilled at making every move thereafter...

Tonight there'll be no debating the master...

After she showed signs that she was willing...

Then I'm fully able....

Ran my hand along her thigh from underneath the table...

The response in her eyes said tonight we won't be watching cable...

We'll create our own scandal...
Her body I'd handle...
As we commence to making erotic shadow puppets in the light from aromatic candles...
Leaned in for her lips...
Light nibble before kiss...
Tongue flavored with wine scents...
Hand tracing skirt slit....
Slight sway of her hips...
All signaled she was ready...
To embark on a trip headed toward bliss...

KP:
He finally got the hint...
And spent...the time...
To send chills up and down my spine...
Replacing the wine, as my intoxicant...
Letting me know that dessert would be much more fulfilling than the meal...
He was a pro at taking it slow...
Which made me want to rush...
Made him blush...
At my bold touch...
Although not prepared...
He wasn't scared...
Simply surprised that I saw no reason to lie...
About my appetite...
Didn't want Diamonds and Pearls...
No trips Around the World...

I just wanted to Get Off....
Tonight...

NP:
My Prince inspired side comes out at night...
As well as in the morning and at noon...
I TRY to use my powers for good...
Bul now I choose to use them to make her swoon...
Excused us from the table...
And moved to the center of the room...
Standing face to face...
Hands upon her waist...
Her ears filled with whispered bass...
"Of U I'd love to taste"....
Dipped to my knees while she stood in place...
I soon was face 2 face....
With red panties composed of lace...
Just finished a gourmet dinner....
But sweet pink is my favorite meal...
Though her knees grew weak I kept her standing...
Until my tongue lashing made her squeal....

KP:
To say that he devoured me...
Would be putting it mildly...
Manhandled me...
Gentlemanly...
Forced me to stand strong...
As he weakened me...

By tasting me...
Repeatedly...
Held my hips...
In a vice like grip...
As he took sips...
Of the juices he caused to drip...
Never tired of the taste...
Yet finally placed me...
On the floor...
Removed his cloth restraints and showed me what was in store...
I smiled and purred...
Beckoned to him and whispered
"What are you waiting for...."

NP:
My clothing may have been removed...
But select pieces of hers remained on...
Because I loved the contrast of her Karmel colored skin....
Against the redness of her bra and thong....
She had one hand in her hair and the other upon her breast...
As I knelt before her....
And held her crossed legs upon my chest....
Nibbled on her ankles...
As I slid her thong to her mid-thigh...
Entered slowly inside her...
Looking into her eyes as she released a sigh...

Her back was slightly arched...

Hips raised to meet my thrusts....

The warmth of her sweet wetness...

Enticed me not to rush....

The feel of the heat upon my thighs from pressing against her behind...

Gave me a feeling of intoxication...

More than I could ever feel...

From partaking of fine wine...

Language of Love

I don't know Spanish Papi
But
I'm willing to learn
The words needed to show how hot my desire burns
For you
My tantalizing
Sensual
Latin lover
With skills that can be matched by no other
As your words move over me
The waves start to crash
My temperature rises
My heart beats fast
Then you touch me
And I begin to shake
We haven't even started yet and the stream is
becoming a lake
But
That's just how good you are
Señor
Doing things that have me begging for more
More of your words
Your touch
Your taste
Even when I close my eyes
I can still see your face
And the fire in your eyes as you do what you do

I don't need to know Spanish to understand you
The language of love needs no translation
Even your smile causes tremors and vibrations
We don't need words to be understood
The oohhs and aahhs are working real good
When I touch you there
I completely understand
That you prefer my kisses to the touch of my hand
Or when I scratch
Shake
And squeeze
You know that what you're doing has me well pleased
We communicate in a way that is as old as time
I understand your needs
You understand mine
No one else needs to understand our intimate conversation
But we both know that the language of love needs no translation

Focus

Can't
Focus
On my
Assignment
Need somebody to get in this ass
I meant
Wait
Ok
What I'm trying to say
Is I want to wet some sheets
And not with study hall ink
Craving to do the natural
Nasty
Get naughty
Don't need to think
Raise your hand to speak
So hot that steam seeps
Like hot ass springs
Fogging up the computer screen
Follow this prompt to my hollow
You better swallow
Fill empty space with more than
Just your tongue
Your grade will be based on participation
With extra points issued
For the various skills you possess
My bodice with

Stay
Focused
Homework
Right
That'll be completed in class
But this
Is NOT a group project
Duets are acceptable
Activities shall be considered
Extracurricular
Once we break a sweat
Maybe pull a muscle or two
Shit
I've got a Charlie Horse
Focus
Girl
Focus
Rather a cramp in your leg
Than fingers
Want you to do me like an open book quiz
Let it be done diving in
Cum take a swim
Rescue me from this fire
Douse me with your hose
Divide then conquer my desire
Like Napoleon
Allow your little men to flow
Focus
Shit

This deadline
Shall be reached
Breached
From behind
Decadence
Run your fingers through my hair
As I straddle you on this computer desk chair
Just one orgasm
Will not improve your grade
Two maybe three might get you a B
But for an A
You need to
Get back down on your knees
This lesson session
You'll thoroughly enjoy
Have me open like a book
And you can pass this test
For sure
All you have to do
Is focus

Cruisin'

Speedin' down a dirt road
Wind in my hair
Suddenly these lights hit me
They just popped up outta nowhere
I thought about gunning it
Putting my foot to the floor
Then figured
What do I need to run for
I know every cop 'round this place
So I found a spot and pulled to the side
And let my fingers slip inside
See
Speed always turns me on
And being still just felt wrong
But when he tapped on the window
And I saw his face
I couldn't help but increase my pace
He opened the door and took my free hand
Gently forcing me to stand
With one hand in his
And the other still in me
I didn't really care what the punishment would be
As long as I reached my destination
With
Or without his help
I was more than capable of getting there by myself
But he had other plans

And placed his night stick in my hand
Smooth and long
I figured
There'd be nothing wrong
With taking it for a little ride
And maybe that tongue too
Yeah
I wouldn't mind seeing what that could do
He must've read my mind
Licked his lips real slow
My knees almost let go
Took the hand that was still at work
Under my skirt
And licked each finger
As if my juices were nectar from the gods
All the while I gripped his rod
One handed
Then he commanded
Me
To turn around
Bent me over my seat
And smacked each cheek
When I reached back
I felt the cuffs click
He said
You have the right to remain silent
But I doubt that you'll be able to manage it
That's when he slid in
And the beating began

It might've been called police brutality
The way he was pounding me
But the only complaint that I can recall
Was that I couldn't jiggle the officer's balls
With my hands cuffed behind my back
He punished my cat
For every imaginable offense
But the only thing that I would confess to
Was being mad when I thought he was through
As we dripped and my legs shook
I thought
I wouldn't mind being a crook
If the one searching me was him
Now
My front seat was fun
But my car wasn't the only one
So
After the cuffs were undone
He carried me to his
Laid me out like a buffet
Then let his tongue have its way
With as much room as that cruiser had
I was still trapped
And he wanted so much more than a snack
There was no point in running
Or resisting
Because no matter which way my hips were twisting
His mouth was right there
Didn't go to Shipley's

But his face was glazed
When he finally released me
I was too dazed
To go very far
Soon the other door opened
And all I could see
Was this one-eyed snake looking at me
Reminded me of his night stick
So I figured I'd take a lick
Then I kissed it
For being so good
It bounced
To show its appreciation
So I kissed it again
Taking time to enjoy the taste
That snake
Must've been part grizzly
From the growls I heard
Then Officer Friendly's hands reached down
First
He held my face
In place
Then he moved lower
And squeezed my nipples
Gently enough to wake up the lioness he had put to
sleep
Yet hard enough for my mouth to need a moment
Teeth reminded him who was in charge

Until his mouth replaced his hands and changed the game
If someone had been counting
They would've been past 65
But not quite to 70
I increased my rhythm and took him deeper in
His tongue stopped
But the growling started again
Then something close to a howl as I abducted his kids
I licked my lips
Kissed his hip
Then looked at him with a smile and said
Baby
That was fun
We haven't role-played in a while

Honeymoon

The time has finally come
We've waited so long
I know you wanted to take your time
But
My desire was too strong
And now
Three rounds later
You throw up your hands and say
Enough
Girl I wasn't ready
You've got some potent stuff
I go to get you some water and a towel to wipe off
the sweat
Thinking to myself
He aint seen nothin' yet
I hand you your water then just watch you with a
smile
You say
I could definitely tell that it's been a while
I let you finish your water then get on the bed on all
fours
I crawl to you slowly and say
Baby
It's time for more
You look like a cornered rabbit with nowhere to hide
I say baby I know you're tired
Lay back and let me ride

At the sound of my voice your soldier comes to full attention

I love having that effect on you

In case I didn't mention

For someone to be tired

You sure took control fast

You said that you had to or else you wouldn't last

I wouldn't mind that

You being quick

The one time you were

You definitely made up for it

From the bed to the floor

Then up against the wall

The bedroom to the living room

We're gonna cover it all

Whether straddling you on the couch or bending over a table

I'll set the tempo whenever you're not able

This is what happens when you tease me and then say I have to wait

You opened that cage and let the beast get out the gate

The only way to cage her again is to make her fall asleep

So I need you to put in work make sure those strokes go deep

Although I think you'll probably want to let her out to play again real soon

We've got a lifetime of this it's just our honeymoon

Fireman

You walk into the room in your work gear
Mumble something that I can barely hear
I ignore you and turn to the window
Give a dismissive wave as I watch the drops flow
You repeat yourself louder
Then wait for my reaction
I turn around and give you a smile of satisfaction
My response is both sexy and quick
I say to you
As I stare at your dick
Cum bend me over and pull my hair
It's raining out so I want to go there
Right now
I want it hard and fast
With you talking dirty and smacking my ass
Maybe later we can switch it up and slow it down
But for now
All I want to hear from you is grunts and smacking
sounds
I want to feel your balls as you crash against my
shore
While I'm screaming
Moaning
And begging for more
Now flip me over and pin me to the bed
While teasing me and giving me just the head
Make me beg for it

Make me fight

So that I can sleep good cum morning light

Make me arch my back to get it all in

Then ram it home again and again

Let me put my legs on your shoulders so you can go deep

I want you to drain me so that all I can do is sleep

Don't stop until you've fucked me dry

Give it to me so good that it makes me want to cry

I want to lose count of the times you make me cum

So that I can't think or move when we're finally done

That's what I want from you

That's what I desire

Now be a good fireman and cum put out this fire

Vanilla Treat

He's the best kept secret in this little town
A white boy who actually knows how to put it down
And wonder of wonders
He's actually packin'
Plus
I've never had better when it comes to tongue
action
I didn't believe it when he said that he could rock
my world
Make my body shake and my toes curl
I figured he was just talking noise
As some men do
And that I would be very disappointed before the
night was through
But that's not what happened
He actually blew my mind
I still get wet when I think about that first time
He started with a dinner that was candle lit
There was soft music playing and wine to sip
At first I thought that part ended a little too soon
Because I still believed that I'd be let down in the
bedroom
Before the bed
He led me to the tub
Then
After the bubble bath
A massage and foot rub

From head to toe
And all points in between
The man had hands like I had never seen
And definitely never felt before
I got greedy and wanted more
I moaned and said please
Enough with the hands
I need you to put it on me until I can't stand
He turned me over and I was surprised
By the exquisite sight that caught my eyes
This wasn't a peppermint but a nice candy cane
I knew that after that night
My views would be changed
I just couldn't believe it so I asked if it was real
He said it's right here you are welcome to feel
Or if you'd like
You can take a taste
We may have all night
But I don't want to waste
Another second
With him in this cold
Put him where you want him
I'll gladly do what I'm told
So I took it in my hands and played with it a bit
Then I moved a little closer and gave the head a
little lick
First my hands said no
Then they said yes
My mouth was too busy to even take a guess

My hands and my mouth couldn't come to a
conclusion
So I decided that my cat had to find the solution
I looked at him and said
I still can't decide
Whether or not it's real
So
You'll just have to slide in this kitten
So that I can see for myself
That it's not just a toy that you took off the shelf
See
I'm already wet
Actually I'm soaked
And if you wanna feel it
This better not be a joke
He said trust me
It's real
Let me remove all doubt
And in one smooth stroke
He was all in
Balls out
I cried out in pain that quickly turned to pleasure
This boy had skills and size beyond measure
When he was done with me I was glad that we
started the night with something to eat
Because if not
I would've passed out long ago from getting his
vanilla treat

Dear Santa

Dear Santa
I've been a naughty girl
I did things to him to make his toes curl
I kissed his tree under the mistletoe
After putting on a sexy private show
We made a video
We used the handcuffs
I kept giving it to him 'til he'd had enough
He enjoyed my naughtiness
At least I think he did
When I finished
He was curled up sleeping like a little kid
When he woke up on that specific day
I was under the tree
The perfect display
No wrapping paper
Just a bow and a smile
I didn't have to tell him things were going to get wild
I pushed him to the couch then did a little dance
That made his head pop out of his pajama pants
He stood at attention like a good soldier should
So I applied a kiss to his morning wood
I hummed Christmas carols while I sucked with all my might
Which is why he has to adjust himself whenever he hears Silent Night
I'm sorry Santa

But it gets much worse after that
I swallowed all his juices then made him lick my cat
See there's just something about making me squirm and moan
That I know really *really* turns him on
And I knew that even after I had sucked him soft
He'd have no problem getting me off
And he did
That man's tongue deserves a gift
My reactions to him had him once again growing stiff
So right there on the living room floor
I worked his pole just a little more
I rode him like the cowgirl that I am
Then we did it doggy style
I know how to please my man
We created new positions to enhance the fun
Used two bottles of whipped cream
We needed more than one
This was by far the best Christmas he's ever had
So
Please forgive me for being so bad
I've been naughty
I admit that it's true
And if you like
I can be naughty for you too

Private Show

I stood at the bar chilling
Taking in the scene
My eyes enjoying the eye candy
Chiseled and lean
There was one on stage
Wearing boots and spurs
Moving in a way that made my kitty purr
I had thoughts of asking for a private show
But how to approach him
I didn't know
As I watched his performance
It seemed to get better
And as it did
I kept getting wetter
I watched the sweat roll as his body glistened
Realizing that a good workout is what I'd been
missing
Since there was no horse near for me to saddle
I figured that this cowboy would be a good thing to
straddle
I watched women reaching for more than his hips
While his shorts bulged with much more than his tips
I wondered if it was real
And if it really worked
If he could get it wet and make me squirt
He stepped off stage as another dancer stepped on

And I figured that my chances of meeting him were gone

To my surprise

He started making his way through the crowd

Skillfully avoiding the hands of those who wanted to know if he was truly well endowed

When he made it to the bar

I offered him a drink

Which he accepted with a sexy smile and a wink

We talked for a while and numbers were exchanged

A time to meet up later was also arranged

I smiled to myself as he made his way back to the stage

Especially when I caught the looks of jealousy and rage

If they had known what I was going to get that night

They would have possibly wanted to fight

We met for a meal and more conversation

Then I learned

With much joy and elation

That he was more than just easy on the eyes

He actually had a brain

What a pleasant surprise

Then from the diner to the hotel room

He did things that had me seeing him as my groom

I mean

A sexy brother with a brain

That knows how to drive a woman insane

Those are hard to come by
Believe me I've looked
So measures to keep this one I quickly took
See
He had me climbing the walls
And god and his name I constantly called
As far as that bulge
It was definitely real
That was proved through taste and feel
His moves on stage were just a tease
That man has skills meant to please
He gave me countless orgasms
More than my fair share
When I tried to run
He gently pulled my hair
To keep me in place until we were both drained
Now I get a kick out of watching these women
making it rain
Because I know that they all fantasize
About touching that bulge between his thighs
But I own the feature
While all they get is a preview
And if you had gotten what I did
You would've cuffed him too

A Good Wife

The bedroom IS undefiled
As long as the connection is blessed
I need to worry about my own
Please him with how I dress
Because men are visual
I need to please his eye
So he's rarely concerned
With the one walking by
So whenever I can
This is what I do
Put on a show
Do a little dance
Put on my stilettos
And prance
Around the bedroom
In some sexy lingerie
Make him forget
Whatever he saw that day
In tight jeans
Or short skirts
Remind him of why
This relationship works
Oh so very well
Take him to Heaven
After he's been through Hell
Because that's what a woman is supposed to do
So that he's never tempted to replace you

Be so pleasing
That temptation can't take hold
Remind him that you're the real deal
And she's just fool's gold
You are his gift
So surprise him every now and then
It's ok to role play
With your husband and best friend
They say a real woman never makes a man weak
I say it's perfectly alright to be his private freak
Make him shake at the thought of your caress
So that he's not worried about how the hood rats dress
Your mark on him doesn't have to be visible
Give him something to think about
That's a good way to keep peace in your home
For everything there is a time and a place
And many different ways to keep a smile on his face
Dressed or undressed
At home or in the streets
You are his sanctuary
In and out of the sheets
So let him find rest
From his stress
But also from his fantasies
Listen to him
Then aim to please

Karmel Coated CooL:
When North Meets South
Collab w/Nathan P.

KP:
The way he wore that suit
It should've been a crime
Simply because of the visions it put in my mind
Like
My unbuttoning his shirt with no hands
Showing him the different ways I can get him to stand
At attention
Make him give me a personal salute
Long before I allow his gun to shoot

NP:
Can I run my fingers thru ur hair....?
Or would u rather finger my pocket square...?
Welcome me with.....
Open arms.....
Open legs.....
And......
An open mind
So many ways 2 play....
So little time 2 grind....
So let's get down to business
Would u like a glass of wine?
Not to drink.....

But to enhance the trip.....
To southern lands.....
Where nature takes a stand.....
Throw a blanket on the floor....
Be sure the lock is on the door....
So I can slide into U from the back....
And work ur inner core...

KP:
I thought
Ever the gentleman
Even in the bedroom
Not knowing the beast would be released soon
I sipped the wine
Then kissed him there
Because
The two tastes I wanted to compare
The wine was good but
His skin was better aged
I released more than ink when I put his pen to my
page

NP:
Even the mildest kitten has moments of Tiger...
Knowing full well I was about to surprise her...
With her Merlot soaked lips....
Introducing me to bliss....
Excuse me miss....
From that glass I must sip...

So that I may embark on my own southern trip....
And allow u to experience...
That Southern Comfort....
NEVER felt like this.....

KP:
Was this northern boy from the NYC
Trying to show southern charm
To me
Movements so fluid that water fumed
Skills so exquisite
I felt consumed
Yet
On my end
I refused to lose focus
I made him disappear
Hocus pocus

NP:
Mathematics was never a favorite subject of mine....
Yet I've always had a love for the #69....
So I felt inclined
As we reclined...
To do the math....
Multiplying the multiples...
As I solved the equation of...
How many licks does it take
To get to the center of a KARMEL pop....

KP:

He spoke in tongues to my pearl

My eyes closed

My head swirled

But

I decided that before I tapped out

I'd let his one eyed head see what my throat was
about

I taught him something he'd never learned in school

And that was this

When she's a headmaster

It's hard to stay Cool

NP:

But it's CooL to stay hard....

So school is in session...

She had this student's...

Full...and undivided attention....

With my slide rule held in the palm of her......tongue

She performed long division.....

Making me squirm....

More than I ever had during any midterm....

All I wanted was to be sentenced to detention....

And continued to be tutored by her personal
attention

KP:

An apt pupil
At least in this class
But
This lesson couldn't last
I finished teaching
His bell rung
I enjoyed the way his head hung
As his knowledge was
Thoroughly drained
I washed him down with the wine
Impatient to start again

NP:
Patience IS a virtue....
But no virtues needed here
She need not wait to start again
Because this cat is always ready....
Impressed with her headmaster's degree....
But alas I possess a PhD...
A Pleasuring her Degree...
Time to show her why she should call me Dr. P

KP:
He looked at me and said
The Dr. is in
It's time for your session to begin
He entered me with surgical precision
Dove deep Into my well
No wishin'

For anesthesia
I wanted to feel it all
I am so glad this Dr. makes house calls

NP:
A full body exam...
Going places a mere intern could never go....
A thorough tongue lashing....
Rounds of deep thrashing....
Nothing can compare...
To my hands-on intensive care...

KP:
Insurance wouldn't cover this Dr.'s bill
So I had to make sure to pay him in thrills
Comprehensive coverage is what my body was given
He had a reputation
Up to which he was livin'
Dr. P couldn't stay cool as various positions were explored
He realized his patient was insatiable
Always wanting more
So his hands and mouth played my body like a flute
Who would've thought that all of that was underneath that suit

NP:

Looks CAN be deceiving....

And ever so pleasing...

She provided full coverage...

So no position was off limits

And that when she made the wise decision...

To retain my as her personal physician

Told her "Tell me where it hurts and I'll be sure to kiss u there...."

And while she pulled me close...

Tongue to tongue

Her fingers in my hair.....

That's when I discovered....

A BETTER pocket for my square...

Whisper

As he
Whispered against my lips
He caused the kind of downpour that could sink
ships
A storm
Yet I was
More than warm
His tongue and mine
Intertwined
As he whispered against my lips
No words
Just quiet commands
That caused me to be unable to stand
Without help
Began to melt
From the heat
As his lips gently beat
Against mine
Whispered in time
With my pulse
The rhythm of my heartbeat matched the tempo of
his whispers
Too weak to fight the feeling
Yet strong enough
And MORE than willing
To talk back
Yet he had tamed this ravenous lioness

With a whisper
Against my lips
Moved my hips
In time
With his whispered flow
To show
My appreciation
And desire
But his
Loud murmurings
Controlled the fire
Always on the verge of ignition
Ready to submit to him
Yet he demanded nothing
Except my lips
To whisper against

Voyeur

I like to watch
Would you like for me to tell you what I see
He
Devouring she
Passionately
Got me squirming in my seat
Wishing it was me
I know I taste sweet
But
It's their juices staining the sheets
Pre-cum
Sweat
I'm shaking and he hasn't even fucked her yet
Damn
How did my hand get wet
Might need to get
A toy
So as to enjoy
The show
Just a lil' mo'
But
I like to watch
And don't want to miss
One kiss
Properly placed
To places
That cause her to make fuck faces

And he STILL hasn't fucked her yet
He's only used his tongue and his fingers to get me
I mean her
Wet
Damn
I bet
He could handle us both
But
I'm only here to watch
As they continue
To do what they do
Her moans
Mingle with my own
As I imagine me in her place
Riding his face
And hands
Damn
I should've paid for the special
Instead of the cheap seats
I've got something for him to taste
I don't want any more to go to waste
But
I only paid to watch
Participation is an extra fee
But I swear he's looking at me
While licking her
He wants me to break the rules
That's not cool
And neither am I

Temp so high
I might cry
If something doesn't happen soon
Maybe if he'd just cum
I could be done
But he's having too much fun
Teasing us both with his tongue
Now I want to do to him what he's doing to her
Let him fuck my mouth while that tongue lashing
continues to occur
If both my mouth and hands were occupied
This heat might finally subside
But then again
I think I'd like to take him for a ride
But I already came from
Wait
No
I only came to
Watch
To get a few thrills
But now
Now I want to test his skills
Shit
They'll just have to send me a bill
And a video

Playtime

his fantasies could never top
My realities
Because he stays
On the bottom
Of my to-do list
My only wish
For him
Is a voyeuristic one
See
I need an audience
Every now and again
So I call my little friend
For a play date
And tell him to watch
But he can't masturbate
Unless I say so
And I won't
I like the way he squirms
As his desire burns
As I and my lover take turns
Pleasing each other
I sometimes wonder
Why he puts up with it
But since I like it
I don't complain
Sometimes I position myself between his knees
As I please

My lover

Mentally

Throbbing from the excitement caused

By his silent applause

And his controlled desire

As I blow on the other's wood

To make a fire

And make his chimney smoke

I may gag

But never choke

Deep throat

My specialty

Especially

While he's watching me

It is

Both privilege and punishment

And he appreciates both

But once I cum

That's all she wrote

I leave them both with hard ons

Tell them to bounce

Because playtime is over and it's time to get out

Speechless

Left me
Speechless
Touched spots others found
Reach less
Caused me to speak
Less
As screams of pleasure
Turned to hoarse murmurings
Had me promising
Everything
Just to feel him again
This had to be a sin
The way he had me calling on the father and the
son
As if he and they were one
In the same
Forgot his and my name
Had me sputtering from both sets of lips
As he slipped
In and out
Then in again
Teasing
Tipping
Gripping
Nipping
My nipples
Causing ripples

That spread from my core

Couldn't even say

More

And I wanted to

Somehow he knew

Because just when I thought we were through

Well

If you were him

What would you do

Unchained

The collar is off
Now it's My time
Playing submissive for so long
Had me losing My mind
Submissiveness
Is just a role
Domination
Is always the goal
Two men in my life
The owner of one
While I'm the other's wife
One likes giving orders
The other likes to receive
Having them both gives me balance
I do believe
I think I'll start with a little tease
Have him face me on his knees
Eyes relaying Mistress please
As I keep Myself just out of reach
he can look but he can't touch
Not until I've had enough
Of watching his desire swell
While I tell
him
Of my submissive games
And my playing as tame
As he is

With me
And I see
his body
React to my voice
It really has no choice
But
I punish him still
For disobeying his Mistress's will
he likes it
And asks for more
As he lets a little pre drop to the floor
Another rule broken
Neither mouth nor dick are to have spoken
So the strap is put away
And he doesn't get to play
Instead
I pleasure myself
While deliberately calling the name of someone else
he gives no reaction
Like a good boy
And goes back to being my favorite toy
As a reward
I give him a taste
Place some Karmel glaze
All over his face
he still can't use his hands
So I stand
While pulling his hair
And letting his tongue take me their

he knows if he can make me weak
he'll get the reward that he seeks
So he works
To make me squirt
Told to lie back
Still no hands
Attempting to stick his tongue inside
As I glide
Across his lips
Finally I let him slip
Inside
And after I take him for one long ride
My need for control has been temporarily satisfied

Drug of Choice

The taste of his skin was all she needed
The lady disappeared with one lick
She became a beast
His personal freak
Ready to do tricks and give treats
As long as she could taste the sweet
Ness
Of him
The way his tongue tasted as they tussled tenderly
Always soothed her
So
Mouth to mouth was required to rejuvenate the
fiend
Touch alone never worked
But once their lips met
She couldn't get
Enough
Of him
Didn't want to come up for air
As she drowned in him
He had no complaints
As her lack of restraint
Excited him
And she
Invited him
To simply enjoy
Be her

Good boy
While she was his bad girl
And let her tongue swirl
All around his skin
Again
And again
From neck
To nipples
To nutts
Never cumming up
For a break
Determined to make him shake
Repeatedly
For no other reason than she
Likes his taste
Licked every line on the tat that ended at his waist
As she moved closer to her goal
That chocolate pole
That always tasted so divine
And had pleased her so many times
French kisses to head
Somehow led
To tonsils being tipped
And shoulders being gripped
While both moaned
Releasing pheromones
Creating their own sensual cologne
Turning each other on
By their actions

She took such satisfaction
In pleasing him
That
As he released
She soaked the sheets
Set off by his taste
Which she always found
So sweet

Motivation

I sent him a sexy pic
So that when his shift ended
He would ignore all invitations
Extended
Except mine
And waste no time
Making his way to me
See
I wanted no misunderstanding
Of my needs
He better hit the drive-thru
Because the only thing I'm serving
Is me
Karmel
Hot and ready
For the taking
I plan on making
The stars pause
To watch the show

I sent him a sexy pic
So he would know
His lady is asleep
And he will be greeted
By his freak
With a private dance
No time for romance

Save the flowers
For the daylight hours
I wanted him to try to resist my powers
I secretly like
When he puts up a fight
'Cause I know he'll give in
As I begin
To taste his skin
Or when
I bend
At the waist
Putting this ass
Right in his face
There's no place
Like home

I sent him a sexy pic
With the caption
I can't wait
And video entitled
Masturbate
His schedule said he got off at 9
He made it home before 8

In Need

Too horny to think
Need someone to drink
From this fountain
Mount and
Do me
Screw me
To the wall
In the hall
Make my legs so weak I have to crawl
Back to the bedroom
Don't know why I feel this way
Maybe it's the full moon
All I know is
I'm too horny to think straight
Can't even masturbate
My toys just frustrate
Me more
Want somebody to make my body soar
And sweat pore
From my skin
As we do it again
And again
And maybe even again
Somebody needs to take a swim
In my pool
I just hope he has strong strokes
This aint no joke

And I
Am too horny to laugh
But I will get mad
If you can't finish what we start
Please play your part
Romeo
Cyrano
Porno
Star
That's what you are
Or rather
What I need
So before you plead
To be the one
Understand that you can't leave
Until I am completely done
Because
I am too horny to care about your needs
See
I've been called insatiable
Greedy
In the bedroom
A straight bully
I have no problem pinning you down
And riding you like a merry-go-round
I promise you'll like it when I go up and down
Round and round
I get off on the sounds
You make

When I take
My time
Blow
Your mind
In more ways than one
And just when you think we're done
I tell you to get on top
See
I'm just too horny to stop
Listen closely
X marks the spot
So
Put my legs in the air
The treasure's right there
That pretty pink pearl
Treat her right
And you might
See my toes curl
As I hurl
Obscenities
Call upon divinities
And squeeze
You
As you please
Me
Repeatedly
How many
Times
Have I cum

Don't know
Lost count
Thinking about tapping out
Still horny
But
We can stop
For now

Curioso

They say
Curiosity killed the cat
But
I am definitely curious about that
Bulge
In his pants
Damn
He can kill this cat anytime
And then revive
With a little mouth to south
See
I'm ready to be turned out
Y'all don't even know what I'm talking about
It's like this
El es muy grande
Comprende
I just wanna take my hand and
See what he's working with
Let me quit
Think about something else
Besides letting him show me his wealth
You know
The family jewels
Looks like he's got the right tools
I mean
The right stuff
To keep me in the buff

Got me wanting to break out the handcuffs
Just so he can handle me rough
Speaking in his native tongue
Dame mas papi
Sí
Me gusta
We can tango
Get tangled
Dancing is nice
But
Naked wrestling is what I really like
He can pin me anytime
I promise I don't mind
We can have a good time
Going round for round
Looks like he can put it down
Cause me to make sounds
Like ooh and aah
Aye Papi
Tomar esta leche
And if he hits it right
I just might
Give him a kiss
That he won't want to miss
Ever again
I will begin
On the tip of his friend
Help him extend
Further

Than he ever has
Pull him past
My tonsils
Looks like he might be a mouth full
See
Yo quiero
What he's got
The thoughts I have keep me hot
When he's around
Solo quiero saber
How he puts it down
Pero no hablo español
Body language is all we have
Entiendes

The Match

There was
So much heat between the lovers
Who were not yet under the covers
That the sun hid behind the clouds
The thunder was afraid to be too loud
All of nature paused
Their breathing not the only sound
Confusing the Richter as they shook the ground
One of them should have been afraid
Two beasts no longer caged
Circling each other
Teeth bared
As claws gripped
Saliva shared
Clothes ripped
Most natural state
Now too late
To throw in the towel
One of them began to growl
Or maybe it was a moan
Some sound of satisfaction
Still hadn't started the action
No need
For speed
Checked their greed
Wanted to savor
The flavors

Created by their labor
One worked with wetness
While the other forged steel
Skin got jealous
Wishing it could feel
What was being tasted
But nothing was wasted
In the overflow
Cleaned up like pros
Didn't miss a drop
Refused to stop
Till the well was dry
And the one eyed snake could no longer cry
No breather
No respite
Not a teaser
But a title fight
With dinner done
The match began
Mouths were now used
For giving commands
Three rounds down
No sign of giving in
Both of them determined to win
He was good
Repeatedly making her shout
But she was the champ and refused to tap out
She held the title
At least in her mind

She wasn't going to lie down
Even if it was round nine
Back and forth
Out and in
Both of them determined to win
But with a groan and a sigh
The match ended in a tie

Showtime

Tickles led to touches
And recess was over
School was now in session
And the real fun was about to begin
Laughs turned to sighs
To moans
To body language that needed no interpretation
Clothes
Which were so cute and comfortable before
Suddenly seemed to be in the way
And although time was on their side
They didn't want to waste a minute
They rushed
Only to take their time
Excited and nervous
Yet confident and sure
Eyes held conversations
That hands translated
Because mouths were busy
Time seemed to stand still
Until
The sun knocked on the window
To let them know the moon had to go
But the sun couldn't hold a candle to their heat
So they continued
Talking tenderly with tongues twisted around
treasures that had been found time and time again

Yet were still

New

They napped like well nursed newborns

And were just as content

Until the hunger returned

Then they began to turn

And turn

Putting on another show for the stars

Any Given Night

Before he even touched me
I was already moist
There was just something about that man's voice
When he talks to me
All low and soft
I start thinking of ways to get him off
I don't care if he's reciting the alphabet
There's something about his voice that always gets
me wet
And he knows it too
So
I'm in trouble
Staying mad at him is a definite struggle
Because all he has to do is give me that sexy smile
Sit at my feet
And just talk awhile
I forget about being mad and get hot instead
Start thinking of ways to get him into bed
Some say that's not good
But it works out alright
Because I have yet to go to bed mad
On any given night

The Many Moods of Me

i'm His good girl when the collar is on
But i can only play submissive for so long
Because the desire to dominate is just too strong
i like the games i play with Sir
AND the number of orgasms that occur
Multiples are always the mission
But
i have to listen
Put my body into submission
And not release until He tells me to
Which is so hard to do
But He makes it worthwhile
If i play along with a smile
Which i do
But
I have my own toys
Good little boys
Who live to please me
Follow my commands
So easily
Born for this
Trained to cum
At a kiss
If I wish
And although I only wear Sir's collar at certain times
They always wear mine
Mentally

No one needs to see
Constantly show that they belong to me
Will stand at attention
At the mention
Of playtime
Can almost read my mind
They love to anticipate
My every whim
Even when they can't participate
See
Sometimes I like to put on a show
And they are the
Perfect audience
They know they can't play
And must stay
Exactly five feet
Eleven and a half inches away
Until I say
Otherwise
And their eyes
Are the only things allowed to leak
Can't speak
Unless told
But
Even being in charge gets old
So
From time to time
When I need to unwind
I find someone I can go back and forth with

Give and get

Affection

Kiss his erection as he frenches my pearl

Takes me around the world

Or the room

Mirrored ceilings give a helluva view

When we do

What we do

Trading

Places

Sex faces

Sweat

And other juices

As they flow free

These are

The Many Moods of Me

www.ingramcontent.com/pod-product-compliance
Lightning Source LLC
Chambersburg PA
CBHW020919090426
42736CB00008B/712